BUSY Little HANDS

ACTIVITIES FOR PRESCHOOLERS

FOOD PLAY!

Amy Palanjian

Hi, KiDS!

This cookbook is for YOU!

You'll find super-yummy recipes that you can
make yourself with a tiny bit of help
from a grown-up.

Remember, clean hands are a must. Before you start
cooking, rub your hands together with soap under
warm water. Wash your hands for at least 30 seconds.
(That's the time it takes you to sing the ABCs twice!)

There are all sorts of fun foods in this book.
Time to put on your apron and dig in!

5 TIPS TO MAKE FOOD MORE FUN

1 Let your hands touch and feel the foods in each recipe.

2 Look for colors and foods you recognize.

3 Taste ingredients as you go.

4 Tell a grown-up about which foods you love and why.

5 Share what you make with family and friends!

Amy

BABY BEAR PORRiDGE

MAKE A FUN FACE IN YOUR INSTANT OATMEAL!

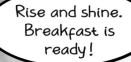

Rise and shine. Breakfast is ready!

GROWN-UP PREP STEPS

Place ¼ cup instant oats, 1 teaspoon hemp seeds, 1 teaspoon maple syrup, and ¼ teaspoon cinnamon in a bowl. Stir in ½ cup of very hot water. Cover with a plate, then let sit for about 3 minutes. Slice a banana into ½-inch slices with the peel on and get out some blueberries or raisins. Let the kids top the oatmeal with milk, if desired, and a fruity bear face.

4

1

Start with a bowl of warm oatmeal.

2

Peel the banana slices.

3

Use fruit to make a silly bear face.

HOO!

What other faces can you make?

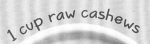

FRUITY BREAKFAST BONBONS

**COOKIES FOR BREAKFAST?
YES, PLEASE!**

1 cup raw cashews

1

Measure out
the cashews, dried
dates, oatmeal, dried
cherries, and water.

1/4 cup water

1/2 cup dried cherries

20 dried dates

GROWN-UP PREP STEPS

Have the kids help you measure the ingredients.
You can use either Medjool (sometimes called
"California") or Deglet Noor pitted dates. Combine
all the ingredients in a food processor and grind
until smooth, stopping to scrape down the sides.
(It will take some time — keep going!) Scoop out
the dough from the food processor. If the batter
is too sticky to roll, chill for 5 to 10 minutes. Store
leftovers in the fridge.

1/4 cup instant oatmeal

6

2

Add the foods to a food processor.

3

Put on the lid and press the button. (It might be loud!) Grind until smooth.

4

Have a grown-up scoop out the dough. Roll into balls. Eat up!

Yum! Yum!

YAY FOR YOGURT BOWLS

STIR UP YOUR OWN YOGURT FLAVORS!

GROWN-UP PREP STEPS

Set out small bowls of stir-ins you have on hand (applesauce, mashed banana, jam, warm nut butter, or puréed peach or squash from a baby food pouch) and toppings (granola, cinnamon, shredded coconut, and chia or hemp seeds). Get out plain yogurt. Let the kids pick and choose stir-ins and toppings to design their own flavored yogurt.

puréed peach

strawberry jam

granola

chia seeds

shredded coconut

8

1
Start with a bowl of plain yogurt.

2
Mix your favorite stir-in into the yogurt.

peach jam

3
Sprinkle on a topping.

Juicy Apple Cobbler

WHAT FLAVORS CAN YOU MAKE?

Berry Patch

Chunky Monkey

applesauce + granola

strawberry jam + fresh berries

peanut butter + mashed banana

OPEN-FACED EGG SANDWICH

MAKE A HARD-COOKED EGG BREAKFAST SANDWICH!

GROWN-UP PREP STEPS

Gather and prep ingredients, including hard-cooked eggs, butter, mayonnaise, mustard, crispy bacon, sliced cheese, sliced ham, and/or baby spinach or lettuce. Get out some slices of your favorite whole-grain bread. Allow the kids to customize their own meals. You can serve this sandwich deconstructed for little kids for easy chewing.

1

Spread butter, mayo, or mustard onto a piece of bread.

2

Crack and peel the hard-cooked eggs.

3

Cut the eggs with an egg slicer.

Watch out for your fingers!

4

Place your favorite sandwich foods on the bread.

bacon

sliced cheese

spinach

egg slices

11

GRAB-AND-GO MORNING MIX

A PERFECT BREAKFAST TO EAT ON THE RUN!

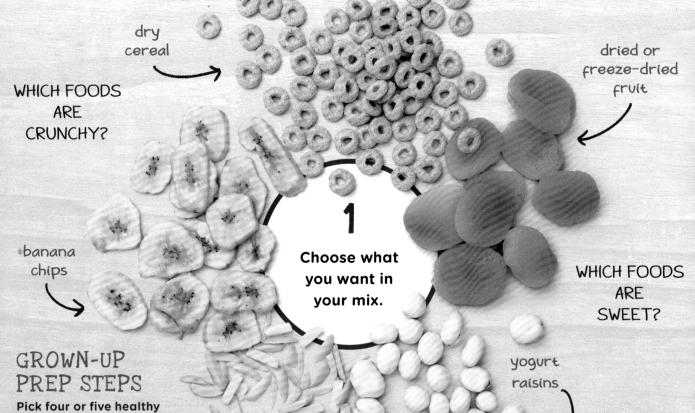

dry cereal

dried or freeze-dried fruit

WHICH FOODS ARE CRUNCHY?

1

Choose what you want in your mix.

banana chips

WHICH FOODS ARE SWEET?

yogurt raisins

GROWN-UP PREP STEPS

Pick four or five healthy trail mix ingredient options, such as dried or freeze-dried fruit, dry cereal, yogurt raisins, banana chips, or sliced nuts for the kids to choose from. Have storage bags or containers ready.

sliced almonds

WHICH ONES TASTE SALTY?

2
Spoon or scoop
your foods into
a bag.

3
Close the bag.
Shake it!

WHERE
WILL YOU
EXPLORE
TODAY?

13

SiLLY SANDWiCH SPiRALS

ROLLED SANDWICHES ARE EASY AND FUN!

GROWN-UP PREP STEPS

Warm a slice of soft whole-grain bread in the microwave for 10 to 15 seconds. Cut off the crusts. Set out fillings for kids to choose from. Have the kids flatten the bread and spread on their filling of choice. Slice sandwiches crosswise into 1-inch sections with a serrated knife.

14

1

Flatten the warm bread with a rolling pin.

cream cheese

hummus

mashed avocado

2

jam

Spread your favorite filling on the bread.

nut butter

3

Roll up your sandwich.

4

Ask a grown-up to cut the sandwiches into spirals.

15

USE-YOUR-NOODLE BOWLS

OODLES OF NOODLES MAKE LUNCH MORE FUN!

1 tablespoon lime juice

1 tablespoon maple syrup

1

Add the peanut butter, lime juice, maple syrup, and soy sauce to a small bowl. Stir together to make peanut sauce.

½ cup creamy peanut butter

2 tablespoons soy sauce

GROWN-UP PREP STEPS

Prepare 8 ounces of rice noodles or spaghetti according to package directions. The recipe makes 4 to 6 servings. Use a vegetable peeler, grater, or spiralizer to make carrot, zucchini, or cucumber noodles. For a nut-free sauce, use sunflower seed butter in place of peanut butter. For a thinner sauce, add ½ cup warm water. Offer toppings such as sesame seeds, diced chicken, tofu cubes, scrambled eggs, or chopped peanuts.

2

Stir the peanut sauce into the veggie noodles and cooked rice noodles.

scrambled eggs

sesame seeds

3

Serve yourself some peanut noodles. Add any toppings you like.

tofu cubes

Noodles too long? Cut them up!

TACO TiME!

PICK AND CHOOSE THE TOPPINGS YOU LIKE!

GROWN-UP PREP STEPS

Drain and rinse a can of black or pinto beans and place in a large bowl. Set out warm soft tortillas, diced avocados, sour cream, shredded cheese, shredded lettuce, chopped tomatoes, and/or salsa and let the kids customize their tacos. The mashed beans will stick more easily to the tortillas, making them easier to eat.

1

Mash the beans with a potato masher.

18

2

Use the back of a spoon to spread the beans on warm tortillas.

shredded lettuce

What toppings will you try?

salsa

shredded cheese

3

Place your favorite toppings on your tacos. Fold and eat!

sour cream

diced avocado

19

SUPERFOODS PLATE

HOW WILL YOU BUILD A HEALTHY MEAL?

PROTEINS · GRAINS · FRUITS · VEGETABLES

chicken · whole-grain crackers · berries · cucumbers

hard-cooked eggs · pita bread · grapes · shredded carrots

cheese · dry cereal · clementines · snap peas

GROWN-UP PREP STEPS

Prepare an assortment of healthy foods for the kids, arranged in core food groups (proteins, grains, fruits, and vegetables) in a muffin tin as shown. Then let the kids pick and choose from each group to build a balanced meal.

20

1
Pick out a plate for your lunch.

2
Choose 1 or 2 foods from each row to put on your plate.

3
Try to get lots of colors on your plate. Eat up!

21

EASY-PEASY PIZZAS

HAVE A PIZZA PARTY AT LUNCHTIME!

THAT TICKLES!

GROWN-UP PREP STEPS

Toast English muffins or mini pita rounds. Then set out toppings such as pizza sauce, pesto, shredded cheese, sliced olives, pepperoni, cooked sausage, bell peppers, broccoli, and pineapple so the kids can do the rest. Warm the finished pizzas in a toaster oven to melt the cheese, if desired.

On top of my pizza, all covered with sauce . . .

1

Use a spoon to spread pizza sauce onto a toasted English muffin.

2

Sprinkle on some cheese.

What other faces do you see on your plates?

3

Use toppings to make funny faces!

sliced olives

pepperoni

shredded cheese

bell pepper

bell pepper

mozzarella

basil

bell pepper

23

GREEN MONSTER MACARONI SALAD

GREEN FOOD IS FUN!

GROWN-UP PREP STEPS

Cook 8 ounces of pasta (like elbows, orecchiette, or wagon wheels) according to package directions. The recipe makes 4 to 6 servings. Warm 2 cups of frozen peas. Work with the kids to stir the rest of the ingredients into the salad.

24

1

Use a crinkle cutter to slice one small cucumber.

What kind of veggies would a green monster like?

1 cup warmed peas

8 ounces cooked pasta

1 cucumber, sliced

2

Measure out the peas, pasta, pesto, mozzarella, and cucumber.

¼ cup pesto

PEAS, please

½ cup mini mozzarella balls

3

Place everything in a large bowl. Stir together!

SANDWICH STICKS

FOOD ON A STICK IS MUCH MORE FUN!

GROWN-UP PREP STEPS

Gather some sandwich ingredient options for the kids to choose from, such as bread cubes, deli meat, cheese slices, hard-cooked eggs, cherry tomatoes, pickles, baby spinach, and lettuce. Also set out a salad dressing, such as ranch or honey mustard. You'll need paper lollipop sticks.

1

Use clean scissors to cut up lettuce and cheese.

26

2

Push your
sandwich fillings,
one at a time,
onto a paper
lollipop stick.

3

Dip your
sandwich
stick into
your favorite
dressing!

Round out your
meal with fruit
and a drink!

HIDE–AND–SEEK SMOOTHIES

VEGGIES ARE HIDING INSIDE!

2 tablespoons mashed avocado

1

Measure out these foods.

1 cup milk

1/3 cup kale or spinach

GROWN-UP PREP STEPS

Have the kids help you prep and measure the ingredients. You'll need to slice and freeze a banana a day in advance. Stay nearby while the kids are using the blender and remind them to wait to turn it on until the lid is on securely. You can even freeze the mixture into a freezer pop mold or serve in a reusable food pouch.

2 tablespoons cocoa powder

2 tablespoons nut or seed butter

1 cup frozen banana slices

28

2

Place the foods into a blender.

3

Put the lid on the blender. Press the button and blend until smooth.

4

Pour your smoothie into a cup. Drink it with a straw or eat it with a spoon.

Can you see or taste the veggies you added?

29

MAGIC MELON JUICE

SMASH UP SOME TASTY JUICE!

GROWN-UP PREP STEPS

Slice up a watermelon, then let the kids cut up the fruit into small cubes, or use a melon baller. Place the watermelon in a gallon-size plastic zip-top bag. Set a small fine-mesh colander over a cup to drain the juice. You can also make this in a blender — just be sure to buy a seedless watermelon!

1

Cut the watermelon into chunks.

2

Place the watermelon in a zip-top bag and seal it. Smoosh and squeeze the fruit with your hands.

You can cut a corner to pour out the fruit.

3

Place a strainer over a cup, then pour in the fruit. Push the fruit with a spoon. Drink up the juice in the cup!

31

SO FUN FLAVORED MILK

STRAWBERRY, CHOCOLATE, BANANA . . . OH MY!

1 tablespoon honey or maple syrup

1

Place the milk, honey, and vanilla in a blender.

1 cup milk

GROWN-UP PREP STEPS

Help kids measure ingredients and let them choose their own flavor, such as cocoa powder or banana. Blend until very smooth, starting on low speed and working up to high.

$\frac{1}{4}$ teaspoon vanilla extract

32

2

Add strawberries, cocoa, or banana to the blender. Put on the lid.

3

Press the button and blend until super smooth!

4

Pour your milk into a cup and drink up!

STRAWBERRY MILK

+

½ cup fresh or freeze-dried strawberries

P.S. Reusable or paper straws are better for the planet than plastic!

CHOCOLATE MILK

+

1 tablespoon cocoa powder

BANANA MILK

+

½ very ripe banana

What flavors can you make?

SHAPE-SORTING STACKERS

PRACTICE SHAPES AT SNACK TIME.

I like little shapes.

HEART

DIAMOND

CIRCLE

SQUARE

TRIANGLE

GROWN-UP PREP STEPS

Gather together cookie cutters in different shapes, soft bread, sliced cheese, and sliced cucumbers. Let the kids cut out shapes and have fun stacking them.

Which shapes do you want to make?

Circles!

Add a layer of hummus for more flavor!

1

Cut out shapes from cheese, bread, and cucumbers.

2

Stack up your shapes!

FUN FRUIT WANDS

MAKE MAGIC AT SNACK TIME.

GROWN-UP PREP STEPS

Wash and prepare strawberries, blueberries, grapes, melon, banana, kiwi, and any other fruits the kids love. Stir together ½ cup plain Greek whole milk yogurt (or nondairy equivalent), juice from half a lemon, ½ teaspoon vanilla extract, and 2 tablespoons maple syrup to make a simple yogurt dip.

Poke a straw through strawberries to remove the stem.

1

Cut up the fruit with a cookie cutter.

2

Push the fruit, one piece at a time, onto paper lollipop sticks.

3

Dip your fruit wand into the yogurt dip and eat.

Make a wish upon a star!

SMASHED AVOCADO TOAST STICKS

HOORAY FOR AVOCADO TOAST!

1

Mash an avocado with your hands in a sealed zip-top bag.

GROWN-UP PREP STEPS

Halve an avocado and remove the pit. Scoop the avocado into a plastic zip-top bag and let the kids mash it with their hands. Lightly toast a slice of bread and then let the kids do the rest! For a sweet variation, try mashed roasted sweet potato instead of avocado and top with cinnamon.

2

Cut a piece of toast into four sticks.

3

Spread avocado on top of the toast sticks.

4

Sprinkle on sesame seeds, shredded cheese, or shredded carrots, if you want.

YO-YO FROYO POPS

HAVE A FREEZER POP PARTY!

GROWN-UP PREP STEPS

This treat requires some waiting since the pops will need to freeze, but the kids can nibble on the fruit while they work. Use enough mangoes or peaches to make 2 cups. Juice half a lemon and use vanilla Greek yogurt. You can also blend the mixture for smoother pops.

1

Cut the fruit into
small pieces. Measure
2 cups into a
large bowl.

2

Add 2 cups of
yogurt and the juice
of half a lemon.
Stir together.

What will
happen when
you put the
yogurt into the
freezer?
(Brrr . . .)

3

Place the fruity
yogurt in freezer pop
molds and freeze for
at least 4 hours.

FROSTED FRUiTY GRAHAMS

DECORATE CRACKERS WITH YOGURT FROSTING!

GROWN-UP PREP STEPS

A clean paintbrush or a small butter knife is an easy tool to help the kids practice spreading. Have the kids spread vanilla Greek yogurt on graham crackers — or try spreading yogurt on watermelon slices, toaster waffles, or toast. Put out toppings like shredded coconut, sprinkles, blueberries, freeze-dried fruit, and mini chocolate chips.

Don't be afraid to get a little messy!

1

Use a clean
paintbrush to paint
yogurt "frosting" on
graham crackers.

2

Sprinkle your
favorite topping
on the yogurt.
Eat up!

Try frosting
a mini
waffle!

How many colors are on your plate?

I see
all colors.

BiG DiPPERS

MELTED CHOCOLATE MAKES SNACK TIME A SLAM DUNK!

whole-wheat crackers

strawberries

kiwi slices

dried apricots

1

Pick and prepare your dippers.

animal crackers

clementine slices

graham crackers

GROWN-UP PREP STEPS

Get everything ready before you start, since the melted chocolate hardens quickly. Have dippers, such as sliced fruit and crackers, and toppings, such as sprinkles or shredded coconut, on hand. Place ¼ cup chocolate chips into a heatproof bowl and microwave in 30-second increments, stirring in between, until creamy. The bowl that melts the chocolate will be warm, so remind kids not to grab it!

2

Poke a piece of fruit
with a fork. Dunk it into
melted chocolate and
place on the plate. Use
your fingers to dip the
edge of a cracker.

3

Sprinkle your favorite
topping on the chocolate.
Wait for the chocolate to
harden, then eat up!

Psst... don't forget to
share your snacks!

COOKIE MONSTER BITES

HERE'S A SWEET AND HEALTHY SNACK TO TRY!

1 teaspoon vanilla extract

1/4 cup slightly warm honey

3/4 cup shredded unsweetened coconut

1

Measure the coconut, raisins, oats, peanut butter, honey, and vanilla into a big bowl.

1/2 cup raisins or dried cherries

2/3 cup slightly warm peanut butter

1 cup instant oats

GROWN-UP PREP STEPS

For a peanut-safe option, substitute sunflower seed butter. This recipe works best if the honey and nut/seed butter are just slightly warm. Be sure to use unsweetened nut/seed butter. If the batter is too sticky to roll, chill it for 5 to 10 minutes.

46

I love cookies.

2

Mix everything together.

Try rolling some in shredded coconut or graham cracker crumbs!

3

Roll the batter into balls.

Add raisin eyes!

47

KIDS' COOKING TOOLS

Here are a few essentials to make time in the kitchen fun and easy for little hands.

paper lollipop sticks

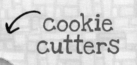

cookie cutters

kids' size rolling pin

safety scissors

crinkle cutter

potato masher

reusable or paper straws

butter knife or kids' knife

PSSST...
GROWN-UPS!

I'm a mom to three kiddos, so I know firsthand how fun (and sometimes challenging!) it is to cook with little kids. These ingredients are accessible and kid-friendly, the steps are supersimple, and everything is either no-cook or no-bake. Plus, the kids get to work their fine and gross motor skills, learn their way around the kitchen, see all sorts of healthy ingredients, and build confidence and independence. So find a time when you're not in a rush and set them up for success with mini cooking tools. Enjoy the process of making and eating food together — no matter how it may turn out!

5 TIPS

FOR GOOD TABLE MANNERS

Get a politeness plan in place
to make table time more pleasant for all.
Say these together:

1

It's okay for us to like different foods.

2

It's okay if we like to eat
the same foods in different ways.

3

It's not nice to "yuck"
someone else's "yum."

4

Before having seconds,
make sure that everyone at the table
has had firsts.

5

Remember to
thank the cook!